Why do most Insurance Agents fail?

How to make a million dollars

In the insurance business

No matter how bad the economy is.

India's No. 1 High Value Insurance Business Coach, Author, Speaker, and Mentor, Randhir Bhalla, shares the success mantra that will make you stand out.

"It always seems impossible until it's done."

\- Nelson Mandela

Randhir Bhalla

NOTION PRESS

NOTION PRESS

India. Singapore. Malaysia.

Dedication

No task is greater than the courage of a man!!!

Loser is the one who didn't fight!!!

This book is dedicated to my students of the "Ultimate Sales Skills" Training Program and to readers of all my books.

Table of Contents

Call To Action

Bonus for early 100 Subscribers

1. Get a straight 30% discount if you are one of the first 100 subscribers.

2. We will provide free mentoring to the first 100 subscribers for a full year.

Please book NOW and Register your Name, City, and Email Address by sending a WhatsApp message or mail on following:

You can connect with Author on
Email: randhirbhalla1950@gmail.com
Mb: +91 9376117563
WhatsApp: +91 9376117563

Preface

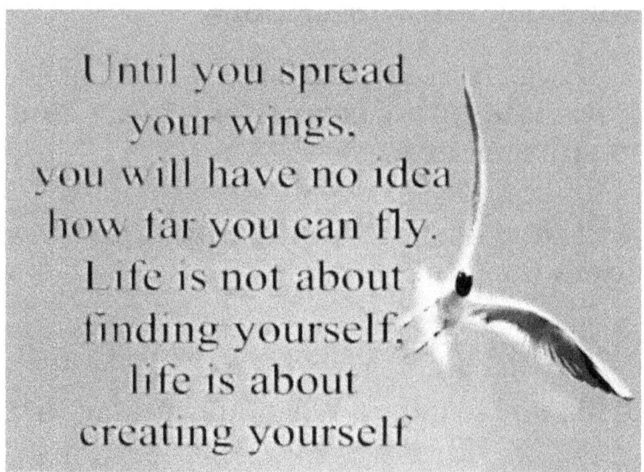

— Napoleon

There's more to this book than its title suggests. This may suggest that the book is only relevant to Insurance professionals. Clearly, this is a fallacy. This book contains ideas and examples that can be useful to anyone who has the grit and resolves to earn a million dollars in his business or profession.

This book dwells around the secrets of earning great success selling insurance and earning as much as 1 million dollars.

The book is a sequel to Author's first 2 books.

To get the most benefit from this book, the author recommends reading his first two books.

It is hard to comprehend how an insurance agent can earn 1 million dollars by selling insurance. As many insurance agents fail to achieve a reasonable level of success in their profession and simply survive by offering large rebates to their clients, this question becomes increasingly relevant.

Having done it himself, the author can vouch for its possibility. This book provides a road map to achieve unprecedented success for even ordinary insurance sellers. In this book, the author claims that following the guidelines and the road map will lead them to incredible success.

Author cautions that while selling big policies to HNIs can certainly contribute to one's financial success, it is important to note that becoming a millionaire further requires giving advice on a combination of factors such as smart financial planning, disciplined savings, investing in the right opportunities, and perhaps most importantly, a long-term perspective. Selling big policies to HNIs can certainly be a part of that equation.

Take a look at this book, read it and experience it for yourself.

Author promises to you that this book is worth a million times more than it is being offered for!!!

Incorporate this book into your sales arsenal. Present this book as a gift to potential clients. He guarantee you will leave an indelible mark on their minds. After all, everyone desires the knowledge to acquire wealth and make a million dollars. The author has achieved this feat successfully, and encourages you to give it a shot and experience the results firsthand.

About the Author

Randhir Bhalla & Associates is a distinguished firm comprising Senior Engineers, Chartered Accountants, and Cost Accountants. Among their accomplished team is Randhir Bhalla, an esteemed author known for his expertise in the field. He has authored three notable books:

1. "6 Secrets of Selling 100 Cr (1 Billion) Insurance to HNIs with Ease": In this book, he shares valuable insights and strategies for effectively selling high-value insurance policies to High Net Worth Individuals (HNIs), enabling readers to navigate this market with confidence and achieve remarkable success.

2. "Sell Big Insurance to Unknown Ferrari Owners": his second book focuses on the niche market of providing comprehensive insurance coverage to owners of luxury vehicles like Ferraris, offering unique perspectives and techniques to capture this specialized segment.

3. "How to Make a Million Dollars in the Insurance Business No Matter How Bad the Economy Is": In this book, he shares his wisdom on achieving financial success in any business, even during challenging economic times. Drawing from his extensive experience, he provides practical advice and strategies to help readers generate significant wealth.

Due to his exceptional knowledge and achievements, he has been invited as a speaker at prestigious events organized by esteemed institutions such as FICCI (Federation of Indian Chambers of Commerce & Industry),

ASSOCHAM (Associated Chambers of Commerce and Industry of India) in New Delhi, and FKCCI (Federation of Karnataka Chambers of Commerce & Industry) in Bengaluru.

Within India, he has earned a reputation as a leading expert in Financial Business Continuity Planning. His customized Financial Business Continuity Plans have proven to be invaluable assets for business enterprises, their promoters, collaborators, investors, and key personnel within organizations. He firmly upholds the belief that Protection (P) always surpasses Returns (R), emphasizing the importance of robust risk transfer mechanisms. With his distinctive approach, he expertly structures comprehensive insurance plans for HNIs, allowing them to mitigate risks effectively and lead stress-free lives.

About the book

This book introduce to the readers a game-changing opportunity. The Author believes it's time to move forward from selling small businesses and embrace the world of Big Ticket Products. The author suggests a revolutionary approach by focussing on providing solutions rather than simply selling products. This transformative book will not only position you as an authority or expert, but also change your life.

Within these pages, you'll find the invaluable wisdom of Mr. Randhir Bhalla, an industry veteran with an impressive 45-year track record working alongside High Net Worth Individuals (HNIs). His unparalleled expertise will guide you on a transformative journey, propelling you from an ordinary insurance seller to an extraordinary force within the industry. Prepare to unlock your true potential and excel in the world of insurance as you absorb his priceless insights.

Chapter-1

This book is a Game Changer

The book has the potential to transform the way readers approach their personal and professional lives. Its ideas and insights can inspire readers to overcome obstacles, pursue their dreams, and achieve unprecedented success.

One of the key messages of the book is the importance of self-belief and having a driving force, or "zunoon," that propels individuals to go after what they truly desire. By following the roadmap provided in the book, readers can discover how to harness their own potential and create a fulfilling life for themselves.

Moreover, the book's relevance extends beyond individual growth and development. Its insights have the potential to benefit the broader community and society by inspiring more people to pursue their passions, contribute to innovation and progress, and make a positive impact on the world.

"You can do anything if you have Self Belief and Zunoon

All your dreams can come true."

- Unknown

Chapter-2

First Things First

Prior to discussing how to become a millionaire in the financial sector, let's understand the following:

1.   There are some of the greatest people in the world who have earned success in their fields. What was their secret to success?

2.   An overview of India's current situation. How the environment is conducive and favourable to the financial sector, including insurance.

3. The growth story of India will continue for decades to come. The insurance industry is here to stay. Don't give up.

Chapter-3

Take a look at what made them reach the pinnacle of success

Through my personal experience and extensive study of biographies of highly successful individuals, I have discovered five common traits that have led to their extraordinary achievements. These traits have served as the foundation for their success and they have shared these insights with their followers.

1.   Be a Risk Taker.

"No Risk No Gain.
Elimination of Risk is a guarantee of failure. "
- Mark Zuckerberg,

Taking Risks is a key trait of highly successful people, as they understand that eliminating Risk is a guarantee of failure. They embrace uncertainty and change, knowing that this is what drives growth and advancement. By taking Risks, they stand out from the majority of people who are Risk-averse, and they are more likely to find success and happiness. In addition, Risk-takers can learn from their failures and apply these lessons to their future decisions.

Taking Risks can open up new opportunities for growth and success. By avoiding Risks, you may be limiting your potential and missing out on potential rewards. While Risks can be intimidating, it is important to weigh the potential benefits and take calculated Risks that align with your goals and values. As Mark Zuckerberg said, the only sure-fire way to fail is to avoid taking Risks altogether

When you take Risks, you open yourself up to new experiences and opportunities. Even if you fail, you'll learn valuable lessons that can help you in future endeavours. This can lead to personal growth and a sense of fulfilment. Research has shown that people who take Risks tend to be more satisfied with their lives, as they have a sense of control over their choices and are more willing to try new things. By embracing Risk-taking, you can become more adaptable and resilient, which can ultimately lead to greater happiness and success.

It's important to note that taking Risks can lead to both success and failure. While selling big insurance policies to HNIs can lead to becoming a millionaire, there is also the Risk of failing to sell those policies.

However, failure should not be feared as it can provide valuable learning experiences and help in identifying areas for improvement. The key is to take calculated Risks, carefully analyzing the potential benefits and drawbacks before taking action. It's important to learn from the failures, have a backup plan in case of failure and to use it as an opportunity to learn and grow. Ultimately, taking Risks is a necessary part of growth and success in any field, including selling insurance policies to High Net Worth Individuals (HNIs).

2. Burn your Bridges.

Long ago, there was a story of a general who was about to face his greatest and most powerful enemy. One who greatly outnumbered his army. He loaded his soldiers into boats, sailed to the enemy's country, unloaded soldiers and equipment, and then gave the order to burn the ships that had carried them.

The general addressed his men before the first battle and said, "You see the boats going up in smoke. That means that we cannot leave these shores alive unless we win! We now have no other choice – we win – or we perish!" They won.

These soldiers didn't have a backup plan. They didn't think to themselves "if anything and I am about to die or we are about to lose we are just going to jump on our ships and go back home to where we are safe and have supper." Instead they gave themselves no choice but to win and they did so because their backs were up against a wall not up against a road they can run back to. And that is the way you need to see your journey.

This story illustrates the importance of burning your bridges, or removing any possibility of retreat or fallback, to achieve success. By eliminating any option of giving up, you are forced to give your all to achieving your goals. This level of commitment and determination is often what separates successful people from those who give up when faced with obstacles or setbacks.

It's important to note that burning your bridges doesn't mean being reckless or not having a backup plan.

"Burn your Bridges" is a metaphorical term that means to eliminate any possibility of going back or giving up on a goal. This can be achieved by fully committing to the pursuit of one's goal. It requires a strong determination and unwavering resolve to succeed, no matter what obstacles or challenges come in the way.

A real life Story of Nawazuddin Siddiqui

The real life story and struggle of Nawazuddin Siddiqui, a successful Indian film actor, greatly inspires me. From a small village in Uttar Pradesh, equipped with a diploma from National School of Drama, he decided to become an actor in the Mumbai film industry. He had no money in his pocket, no friends, and no contacts in the city. His dark skin, lean physique, and short stature make him look like a typical villager. In Bollywood, such personality would not be encouraged. For ten good years, he struggled. Despite doing odd jobs and remaining hungry for days on end, he never gave up on his dreams.

A back-up plan was not on his mind, he said. It was a firm resolve to stay in Mumbai and keep trying for a break in the film industry, even if it took 20-30 years."

As a result, he had truly burned his bridges. A person with that kind of steely resolve would even win the favor of God.

Take a look at this person. He is one of the most successful and wealthy film artists in Bollywood.

Burning your bridges has this power.

"Burning bridges" can be a powerful tool in achieving success as it eliminates the possibility of looking back or giving up. It requires a strong mindset, unwavering determination, and a willingness to take Risks and face challenges head-on.

3. Be a Self Motivator.

Make your own identity. "No one can motivate you, until you motivate yourself." Some people immediately implement their thoughts and ideas because they are self-motivated; this is a combination of self-motivation and planning and can give you desired results to be successful.

Being self-motivated also means **having enough self-awareness to know what works for you and what doesn't**. Rather than depending on others to give you a reason for doing, your sense of motivation comes from within. Your drive comes from your interests, values, and passions, not someone else's checklist.

All successful people are self motivated. They don't depend on external environment for availing a source of inspiration. They compete with themselves and not with others. They set their goals clearly and perceived them relentlessly until they succeed.

4. Break your Glass Ceilings.

"Irrespective of the barrier that you might be facing in your real life, you need to perceive your goal with a single minded purpose. You will soon find the glass ceiling vanish in the thin air."

-   Unknown

Breaking your glass ceiling means overcoming any barriers or obstacles that prevent you from reaching your full potential or rising to senior positions. It involves identifying and challenging societal norms or institutional biases that limit your progress in your career or personal life. By breaking your glass ceiling, you can achieve your dreams and aspirations, regardless of any limitations imposed upon you. This requires having a strong sense of self-awareness and self-confidence, as well as a willingness to take Risks and challenge the status quo. It may also involve seeking out mentors, allies, and other sources of support to help you navigate your path towards success.

Breaking the glass ceiling is relevant to selling big policies to HNIs because it requires going beyond one's comfort zone and pushing oneself to achieve higher levels of success. The glass ceiling refers to the invisible barrier that prevents women and minorities from reaching top positions in their profession or industry. Similarly, selling big policies to HNIs requires breaking through mental barriers and limitations that prevent one from reaching the highest levels of success in the industry. By breaking through these barriers, one can achieve unprecedented success and reach new heights in their career. It requires taking Risks, being self-motivated, and continuously upgrading one's skills to reach the top of the industry.

5.   Trust your own wings

The phrase "Trust your own wings" means to have confidence in yourself and your abilities to achieve success, instead of relying on others to help you. It encourages individuals to take responsibility for their own lives and pursue their goals with self-reliance and determination. The idea is that just as a bird trusts its own wings to fly, you should trust in your own strengths and capabilities to reach your aspirations.

I am deeply inspired by the chapter "Trust your own wings" published in Economic Times under the column Speaking Tree. I am reproducing this. Take a look at it.

"Many of us are fraught with peer pressure, examination pressure and emotional turmoil from

life- changing events. In many colleges and cultures, students have at some point made fun of certain peers by calling them geeks or nerds, for example. But they are often the ones who turned into Bill Gates and Steve Jobs, Thomas Edison and Albert Einstein. They were the ones who left us with great discoveries and insights.

Krishn says in the Bhagwad Gita, 'Man is made by his belief. As he believes, so he is.'

As a young man, it is said that Gandhiji used to hang around with friends who were neither regular with their studies nor interested in a meaningful life. This really bothered his mother, Putlibai. 'Mohan,' she said to him once, 'I have asked you so many times not to hang out with those boys. You will become like them. I can't bear the thought of seeing you smoke or drink.'

Gandhi laughed and said, 'Mother, stop worrying. I don't go around with them so I may become like them. Instead, I do that so they may become like me. Have faith in me. Nothing can deviate me from my path.' And, it is said that Gandhiji did gradually transform his peers.

A strong mind never sways for everything. At the end of the day, what matters is what we really want to do with our lives.
No one can force us. If people around us are like the river, we can become the ocean.

Everyone respects strength. A bird sitting on a tree is never afraid of the branch breaking, because her trust is placed not on the branch but on its own wings."

- Source: ET, Speaking Tree, Jan 27, 2023

Achieving greatness often involves navigating obstacles, setbacks, and distractions. What sets great achievers apart is their ability to persevere and maintain their focus on their goals despite these challenges.

While it's true that great achievers possess an unwavering belief in them and maintain focus on their goals, they are not immune to distractions or external forces. Instead, they develop strategies to overcome these challenges and continue to work toward their objectives.

Summary:

The chapter discusses five common traits that successful people possess: Being a Risk-taker, Burning Bridges, Being a Self-Motivator, Breaking Glass Ceilings, and Trusting your own Wings. These traits serve as the foundation for extraordinary achievements and success in any field, including selling big policies to HNIs. By embracing these traits, individuals can develop a strong sense of determination, perseverance, and resilience, ultimately leading to greater happiness and success. Additionally, the chapter provides real-life examples and quotes to illustrate the importance of each trait and how it can be applied to achieve success.

Chapter-4

The Current Scenario

Why do most Insurance Agents fail?

The current state of the insurance industry in India is concerning, with only about 1% of the approximately 19 lakh (1.9 Million) insurance agents qualifying for MDRT (Million Dollar Round Table), which is the first level of success. Even among those who do qualify, only handfuls are able to achieve respectable earnings. This raises the important question as to why such a large proportion of agents are unable to even reach the first rung of success. It is no surprise that insurance penetration in the country is extremely low. Clearly, something needs to be done to address this issue. In this chapter, the author analyzes the reasons for this state of affairs and proposes potential solutions to remedy the situation.

One contributing factor to the high failure rate among insurance agents is the low barrier to entry into the industry. This can lead agents to believe that they don't need to invest in their business to be successful, which ultimately results in failure.

The reality is that the insurance industry is just like any other business.

That's right. Just like any other business, success in the insurance industry requires hard work, dedication, and a willingness to invest in your business. Unfortunately, many insurance agents enter the industry with the misconception that it's an easy way to make money without much effort. This mindset can lead to a lack of investment in their business, including in training, marketing, and building relationships with clients. As a result, many insurance agents struggle to find success and end up leaving the industry.

In today's digital age, traditional methods of generating leads and acquiring clients are no longer enough to succeed in the insurance industry. Insurance agents need to embrace modern, advanced tactics to scale their business and stay ahead of the competition. This includes utilizing digital marketing strategies, such as search engine optimization, social media marketing, and email marketing, as well as leveraging data and analytics to make informed business decisions. It's important for insurance agents to stay up to date with the latest technology and trends in order to effectively market themselves and provide value to their clients. By doing so, they can increase their chances of success and achieve their business goals.

They have not burned their own bridges.

A large number of insurance advisors work part-time and are not fully committed to their jobs. It is about such people that the story described in the earlier chapter "Burn your Bridges" is about. Clearly, they lack conviction and self-belief. It is important to them to have a safety net in case they do not succeed at their jobs. In other words, they haven't burned their bridges and prefer to ride on two horses. One of the major reasons why a large chunk of insurance advisors fail is because of this.

Summary:

The chapter discusses the current state of the insurance industry in India, with only a small percentage of insurance agents achieving success. One contributing factor to this is the low barrier to entry, which can lead to a lack of investment in training, marketing, and building relationships with clients. Insurance agents need to embrace modern digital marketing strategies and stay up to date with the latest technology and trends to succeed in the industry. Additionally, a large number of insurance advisors work part-time and are not fully committed to their jobs, lacking conviction and self-belief. It is important for insurance agents to fully commit to their jobs and burn their bridges to increase their chances of success.

Chapter-5

Is the career of insurance agents facing significant Risks?

Are you familiar with these challenges and potential Resolutions?

What are the Threats & Opportunities for Insurance Agents?

Threats:

1. Does the insurance industry provide a level playing field for agents, online sales platforms and aggregators?

"PolicyBazaarFintech, an online Insurance aggregator said 4,000 companies have taken employee insurance and around 25,000 firms have taken some kind of insurance product from it."

Source: ET News, 12th June 2023

Online sales platforms and aggregators are permitted to sell products from multiple companies at significantly lower prices and better commissions than what a traditional insurance agent can offer, it raises questions about the fairness and level playing field within the industry.

With the help of state of Art technology, deeper reach and pockets full of money to burn around in order to grab the largest share of the market, these companies are posing a bigger threat to the community of insurance agents.

One of the biggest threats to Insurance agents is lack of adaption of state of art technology.

The artificial intelligence has got a big role to play. Just for example the recent report from HDFC bank says as under
"Your personal unsecured loan will be processed within the count of 1 to 10, regardless of whether you are a current client of the bank or not."

The organized insurance sellers will have an edge in this regard as they will be better off in terms of providing not only cheaper products but also transparency and speed of execution. . Failing to adopt such technologies could put insurance agents at a significant disadvantage and hinder their ability to remain competitive in the rapidly changing insurance industry.

2. How to sell large policies with premiums exceeding Rs. 5.00 Lacs post April 1st, 2023?

The recent changes in tax laws, introduced by the Union Budget, have created a disadvantage for selling large policies with premiums over Rs. 5.00 Lacs, as these policies will lose the tax benefits under Section

10(10)D. This raises the question of how one can sell sizable policies to HNIs.

Opportunities:

Despite the challenges posed by insurance aggregators and online insurance selling platforms, insurance agents in India can still have a promising future by adapting to the changing landscape and focusing on their unique strengths. Here are some key factors that can contribute to the future success of insurance agents in India:

Embracing technology: Insurance agents can adopt digital tools and technologies to streamline their operations, improve customer interactions, and expand their reach. This may include using customer relationship management (CRM) systems, social media marketing, mobile apps, and online portals to better serve customers and compete with digital platforms.

Personalized service and advice: One of the key strengths of insurance agents is their ability to provide personalized advice and build trust with customers. By focusing on this aspect, agents can differentiate themselves from online platforms and aggregators, which may lack the human touch that some customers still value.

Niche markets and products: Insurance agents can focus on specific niche markets or product segments where their expertise and personalized approach can add more value than digital platforms. This could include serving high-net-worth individuals, or clients with specialized insurance needs.

Collaboration with online platforms: Instead of competing directly with online platforms and aggregators, insurance agents can explore partnerships and collaboration opportunities. This could involve working as local representatives for online platforms, providing on-the-ground support, or offering complementary services.

Continuous professional development: Insurance agents can invest in their professional development by acquiring new skills, certifications, and industry knowledge. This will help them stay relevant in the evolving insurance market and provide better value to their clients.

Focus on customer experience: By prioritizing customer satisfaction and providing exceptional service, insurance agents can build long-term relationships with their clients, leading to repeat business and referrals.

Regulatory support: As mentioned earlier, regulators can play a vital role in creating a level playing field between insurance agents, aggregators, and online platforms. By ensuring that regulations are fair and consistent across all channels, regulators can help agents remain competitive in the market.

Summary:

The career of insurance agents in India is facing significant risks due to the changing landscape of the industry. One of the biggest challenges is the lack of adaptation to state-of-the-art technology, which can put insurance agents at a disadvantage compared to organized insurance sellers who can provide cheaper products, transparency, and speed of execution.

Furthermore, insurance agents are raising questions about the fairness and level playing field within the industry, as online sales platforms and aggregators offer lower-priced insurance products with better commissions than traditional insurance agents.

Another threat to insurance agents is the recent changes in tax laws, which have created a disadvantage for selling large policies with premiums exceeding Rs. 5.00 Lacs as these policies will lose the tax benefits under Section 10(10)D. This poses a challenge for selling sizable policies to high net worth individuals.

In conclusion, while insurance agents in India face challenges from insurance aggregators and online platforms, they can adapt and thrive by leveraging their unique strengths and embracing the opportunities presented by technology and collaboration. By doing so, they can continue to play a crucial role in India's insurance ecosystem.

Chapter-6

The Shining India

Look at the level of optimism all around us.

"The Indian economy has undergone a large structural shift in the last eight years and is currently the 5th largest economy in the world after overtaking the United Kingdom. Going ahead, India is expected to pip Germany in 2027 and Japan by 2029 at the current rate of growth, as per a State Bank of India (SBI) research report."

Source: ET, Sep 03, 2022

"India is a shining star amid global economic uncertainty: Christian Sewing, CEO, Deutsche Bank

India will be the 'shining star' of the global economy that faces a decade of volatility amid war, inflation and supply chain disruptions, although New Delhi could make implementation of projects easier to attract more overseas investments, Christian Sewing, CEO, Deutsche Bank, told ET."

Source: ET, Oct 03, 2022,

Why Morgan Stanley believes the next decade is India's?

"India is now the 3rd largest economy in the world in PPP (Purchasing Power Parity). From this, higher base 6.5 % growth looks impressive. Morgan Stanley thinks India will account for no less than 25% of world GDP growth in the next decade.

For the first time, a major investment bank forecasts that India will become a locomotive of the world economy. Quite a change from being world's biggest beggar (India was once No.1 beggar for foreign and food aid)".

Says Swaminathan S Anklesaria Aiyar – Economist

"In 50 years, I have never been so optimistic about India. The best time for India is about to come. We are further going to add maximum nos. to the middle class and our domestic consumption will drive growth."

Says Deepak Parekh - Chairman HDFC Ltd.

"The World Bank and IMF maintain a positive outlook on India's economy. There are several key reasons for this optimism surrounding India's economic prospects. While the global economy is experiencing a slowdown, with the US GDP dropping from 1.8% to 1%, China's GDP falling from 10% to 6% and further declining to 3%, and Europe facing a recession, India stands out as a beacon of growth with its GDP expanding at a rate of 6-7%. This growth, fueled by increasing consumer demand, is attracting a significant number of foreign investors to the country.

One of India's most significant assets is its youthful population. It is projected that in the coming years, 22 out of every 1000 working individuals worldwide will be Indian. The country benefits from a demographic advantage, as the median age of its population is only 29.

The Indian economy is also bolstered by a robust democratic system, a stable government, and transparent policies. A mere 0.5% increase in exports could lead to a 4% rise in India's GDP growth. It is expected that India will become the world's third-largest economy within five years.

Furthermore, India is on the verge of transitioning to positive real interest rates, which is another encouraging economic indicator. The Reserve Bank of India (RBI) has been praised for its effective management of macroeconomic stability.

In summary, with these factors in play, India is poised to experience significant economic growth and prosperity in the coming decades."

- Aditya PuriAditya Puri, Former Chief Executive of HDFC Bank.

India's growth is driven by factors such as an expanding middle class, a robust start-up ecosystem, and increased foreign investment. By 2030, the number of middle-class income earners is projected to rise to 140 million, and the number of HNIs to 14 million. Additionally, India's per capita income is expected to rise from $2,500 to $10,000 in the next decade, increasing disposable income for financial products like insurance and investments.

Political stability and proactive policy measures have attracted foreign investments, and India is becoming a preferred alternative manufacturing location to China. Social security coverage is also expected to expand through insurance products.

India's start-up ecosystem has seen an impressive rise in the number of unicorns, with the country now ranking as the third-largest start-up economy globally, behind the US and China. The growth of Indian unicorns can be attributed to factors such as a large consumer market, increased internet penetration, supportive government policies, and a strong investor environment. Examples of successful Indian unicorns include Flipkart, Paytm, OYO Rooms, and Byju's.

These start-up founders often come from middle and lower-class backgrounds, showcasing the immense opportunities that exist in the financial sector, with the insurance sector poised to benefit greatly. To succeed in this environment, individuals must maintain self-confidence and utilize modern techniques.

India's rapid growth is also demonstrated by the creation of a new billionaire every two days and the addition of 70 new millionaires every day. However, this wealth concentration has raised concerns about inequality and its impact on society.

India's growth story is undoubtedly a long-term one, spanning across decades, and offers numerous opportunities for individuals and businesses alike.

"The people who are crazy enough to think they can change the world are the ones who do."

-   **Steve Jobs**

Summary:

The Indian economy is expected to continue to grow and become a dominant player in the global economy, with projections that it will overtake Germany and Japan in the coming years. The increase in per capita income and the rise of the middle class will result in more disposable income and a greater demand for financial products such as insurance and investments. The Indian start-up ecosystem has seen significant growth, with over 100 unicorns and a thriving investor environment. However, there is also wealth inequality, with a concentration of wealth in the hands of a few individuals. The long-term potential of India remains promising, and success will require hard work, dedication, and the use of modern techniques.

Chapter-7

The Path To Becoming A Millionaire - Unending Opportunities

Smartly optimize your resources and redefine your target market segment.

In the coming years, the Indian billionaires club is expected to grow exponentially, but will everyone benefit from this progress? Although optimism is prevalent, not everyone is reaping the rewards. The choice of market segment plays a crucial role in determining whether or not one is a part of India's all-around growth. Now is the time to redefine your segment.

Why should you focus on the HNI segment when selling high-value insurance policies? The world has changed since the Covid-19 outbreak. Wealthy individuals have grown wealthier, while the poor have become poorer.

In 2021, 84% of households in India experienced a decline in income. However, during the same period, the number of Indian billionaires increased from 102 to 187, as indicated by the 2023 M3M Hurun Global Rich List and Oxfam report. This highlights the stark income divide exacerbated by the pandemic. India now ranks third globally in terms of billionaires, following the USA and China.

Indian billionaires are among the wealthiest individuals worldwide in five different sectors, including technology, energy and natural resources, infrastructure, pharmaceuticals and healthcare, and retail.

The rich have become extraordinarily richer. The world has witnessed an unprecedented number of billionaires in the past year. Because of the sudden rise in their income and the vulnerable global economy, wealthy individuals are experiencing growing financial insecurity and seeking risk management tools to protect their wealth.

Post Covid-19, HNIs are increasingly concerned about potential losses as a result of sudden untimely permanent departure on account of death and are more inclined to manage Succession Risk.

As a result, we have a great opportunity to assist high net worth individuals by mitigating their unresolved personal pains and threats.

With limited resources available, it is crucial to optimize them and focus on this growing market segment.

How do I look at this assorted piece of information?

Interpreting this diverse information, it's evident that a significant opportunity lies ahead. While 84% of households have experienced a decline in income, 16% of the population has grown wealthier. This equates to approximately 22.4 crore people (about 70% of the US population) reaping the benefits of India's growth, comparable to over two-thirds of Americans.

As their incomes, lifestyles, and spending habits evolve, these individuals require risk mitigation tools to preserve and enhance their wealth. This segment is large enough to warrant special attention, and even capturing a small market share of it can lead to significant personal success.

In essence, focusing on this growing segment is a strategic way to optimize limited resources and seize the opportunities presented by India's thriving economy.

Additionally to what has been mentioned above, focusing on the high net-worth individual (HNI) segment is important for selling high-value insurance policies for several reasons:

Affordability: HNIs have the financial resources to afford high-value insurance policies. They are more likely to invest in premium insurance products that offer extensive coverage, ensuring their assets and lifestyle are well protected.

Customization and complexity: High-value insurance policies often require a higher level of customization to meet the unique needs of HNIs. These individuals may have diverse and complex financial portfolios that include multiple properties, businesses, and other valuable assets. Focusing on the HNI segment allows insurance companies to develop specialized policies that cater to these specific needs.

Risk management: HNIs often have a higher Risk exposure due to their extensive assets and lifestyle choices. As a result, they require comprehensive insurance policies that can adequately manage these Risks and provide financial protection in case of unforeseen events.

Profitability: High-value insurance policies typically have higher premiums, which can generate substantial revenue for insurance agents. By focusing on the HNI segment, insurers can increase their profitability and enhance their financial performance.

Cross-selling opportunities: HNIs often have multiple insurance needs, ranging from life insurance and health insurance to property, liability, and business insurance. By targeting this segment, insurance agents can cross-sell various products and services.

Brand reputation: Successfully catering to the HNI segment can elevate an insurance agent's brand reputation, positioning them as a premium provider of insurance products and services. This can help attract additional high-value clients and enhance the company's overall market position.

Relationship building: HNIs often value personalized service and long-term relationships with their insurance providers. By focusing on this segment, insurance agents can develop deeper connections with their clients, leading to increased customer loyalty and retention.

In nutshell, targeting the HNI segment for high-value insurance policies is crucial due to their financial resources, complex insurance needs, and the potential for increased profitability and stronger customer relationships.

Summary:

The chapter highlights the current state of the Indian economy, which is expected to continue growing rapidly in the coming years, creating opportunities for individuals to become wealthy. The chapter suggests that individuals should focus on selling high-value insurance policies to the high net-worth individual (HNI) segment to optimize their resources and increase their chances of becoming a millionaire. The HNI segment is more likely to invest in premium insurance products and require specialized policies to cater to their diverse and complex financial portfolios. Targeting this segment can lead to increased profitability, cross-selling opportunities, and stronger customer relationships. It also emphasizes the importance of keeping up with modern techniques and utilizing digital marketing strategies to succeed in the insurance industry

Chapter-8

Likes and dislikes of HNIS while buying insurance policies

High net worth individuals (HNIs) have unique preferences and expectations when it comes to purchasing insurance policies. Here are some common likes and dislikes of HNIs while buying insurance:

Likes:

Customization: HNIs appreciate insurance policies that are tailored to their specific needs, risk profiles, and financial goals. They expect personalized coverage that addresses their unique circumstances, such as insuring high-value assets, covering liabilities related to their businesses, or providing for their families.

Expert advice: HNIs value the guidance of knowledgeable insurance advisors who understand the complexities of their financial situations and can recommend suitable insurance products and strategies. They appreciate advisors who can provide insights into tax implications, estate planning, and asset protection.

Discretion and privacy: HNIs often have concerns about privacy and confidentiality when it comes to their financial affairs. They prefer dealing with insurance providers who can guarantee discretion and ensure that their personal information remains secure.

Exceptional service: HNIs expect high levels of service and support, with dedicated advisors who are responsive, attentive, and available to address their concerns or answer questions. They appreciate a seamless customer experience that reflects the premium nature of the insurance products they are purchasing.

Comprehensive coverage: HNIs prefer insurance policies that provide comprehensive coverage, protecting their wealth from a wide range of risks. This may include coverage for institutional secured liabilities, director's personal guarantees, multiple homes, luxury vehicles, private jets, yachts, valuable art collections, and more.

Dislikes:

Standardized policies: HNIs typically have little interest in off-the-shelf insurance products, as these often do not cater to their unique needs and circumstances. They seek customized solutions that can address their specific requirements and risk profiles.

Inexperienced advisors: HNIs may be wary of insurance advisors who lack experience or expertise in dealing with high net worth clients. They prefer to work with professionals who have a proven track record of serving affluent individuals and understand the nuances of their financial situations.

Lack of transparency: HNIs dislike insurance policies that are not transparent in terms of coverage, exclusions, fees, and charges. They appreciate clear and concise policy documents and explanations to ensure they fully understand the terms and conditions.

Inefficient communication: HNIs expect prompt and efficient communication from their insurance providers. Delays in response times or failure to provide timely updates can lead to dissatisfaction and potentially harm the business relationship.

Aggressive sales tactics: HNIs generally dislike high-pressure sales tactics or being pushed into purchasing insurance products that may not align with their needs and goals. They prefer a consultative approach where their concerns and preferences are carefully considered.

Understanding the likes and dislikes of HNIs can help insurance providers better tailor their products, services, and sales strategies to meet the unique needs and expectations of this affluent clientele.

Summary:

High net worth individuals (HNIs) have distinct preferences when purchasing insurance policies. They appreciate customized solutions, expert advice, discretion, exceptional service, and comprehensive coverage. On the other hand, they dislike standardized policies, inexperienced advisors, lack of transparency, inefficient communication, and aggressive sales tactics. Catering to HNIs' unique needs and expectations can help insurance providers create tailored products and services that effectively serve this affluent clientele.

Chapter-9

The insurance business is here to stay. You Just Can't Give Up!!!

"Life Insurance Selling Companies collected 17% less premiums in February 2023 than they did in February 2022."

Source: ET, 11th Mar 2023.

Don't be discouraged by such news. Even with such adverse news, the life insurance industry has a bright future.

Take a look at the positive aspect of the same news item.

"Premiums collected by insurance companies increased by 25.06 % in 2022-2023."

Any industry would be pleased to see such substantial growth.

India is a young nation. As of now, the average age of an Indian is only **29**. According to estimates, it will only reach **35** by 2050.

As their income grows, they will look forward to purchasing Life Insurance policies to protect their financial futures.

There is no doubt that India is a bright spot in the world.

 Never give up !!!

Just keep on sharpening your saw by learning new techniques and methods.

Summary:

The life insurance industry in India experienced a 17% decline in premiums in February 2023 compared to the same period in the previous year. However, the overall premiums collected by insurance companies increased by 25.06% in 2022-2023. Despite the temporary setbacks, the future of the life insurance industry in India is bright, given the country's young population and growing incomes. Insurance agents should not be discouraged by the occasional negative news and should continue to learn and improve their skills to succeed in the industry.

Chapter-10

Growth Prospects for the Life Insurance Industry

New Insurance Premium of Life Insurance Sector may Grow At 19% over 4 Fiscals

High GDP growth, rising income, bigger shares (63%) of younger population aged 15-59, focussed on Financial inclusion, preference towards savings with more financial literacy, and increasing adoption of insurance through digital channels are all expected to propel the growth of India's Life Insurance sector.

Source: 17th Feb, 2023, Business Times.

New Business Premium over FY 22-27 E (in Rbn)

Year	Annual Premium	CAGR
FY 17	1750	12%
FY 18	1939	12%
FY 19	2147	12%
FY 20	2589	12%
FY 21	2783	12%
FY 22	3143	12%
FY 27 E	7500	19%

It is my firm belief that those who remain in the insurance business patiently and continuously upgrade their skill levels to deal with selling high value insurance to HNIs will soon become extremely wealthy.

This is the best time in history to be alive. More wealth is being created in more ways all over the world than never before. Despite calamities like Covid and Ukraine wars, the Rich have become richer across the world.

It is important to remember that they are all potential clients.

Chapter-11

Leadership Not a Monopoly of the Well-Educated:

Is it necessary to be well-educated to succeed in business?

No, having a formal education is not a necessary requirement to succeed in business. Many successful business leaders and entrepreneurs did not have a college degree, and instead, they relied on their creativity, ingenuity, and hard work to achieve success.

That being said, having a formal education can provide individuals with the skills, knowledge, and network needed to succeed in business. A college degree or specialized training can help individuals develop critical thinking, problem-solving, and communication skills, as well as provide them with a foundation in finance, marketing, and other essential areas of business.

Ultimately, success in business depends on a variety of factors, including hard work, creativity, determination, and a willingness to take Risks. While education can be helpful, it is not the only path to success.

Success stories of businessmen without college degrees

There are many successful businessmen, who did not have a college degree, including:

Steve Jobs: The co-founder of Apple dropped out of Reed College after just one semester but went on to become one of the most successful and innovative entrepreneurs of his time.

Richard Branson: The founder of Virgin Group dropped out of school at age 16 and started his first business, a student magazine, before launching Virgin Records and a host of other successful ventures.

Michael Dell: The founder of Dell Computers started his business in his college dorm room, but he never graduated from the University of Texas.

Henry Ford: The founder of Ford Motor Company did not attend college but went on to revolutionize the automotive industry with his innovative assembly line production techniques.

Ingvar Kamprad: The founder of IKEA left school at age 17 and started selling matches and Christmas decorations before building one of the world's most successful furniture companies.

Dhirubhai Ambani: The founder of Reliance Industries, one of India's largest conglomerates, dropped out of school after 12th grade and started his business career as a gas station attendant.

Karsanbhai Patel: The founder of Nirma, a leading manufacturer of detergents and soaps, did not attend college and started his business with just Rs. 5000 in savings.

Gautam Adani: The founder of Adani Group, a diversified conglomerate with interests in ports, logistics, power, and infrastructure, dropped out of college in his second year and started his business career as a diamond sorter.

Subhash Chandra: The founder of Essel Group, a leading media and entertainment company, did not attend college and started his career selling rice.

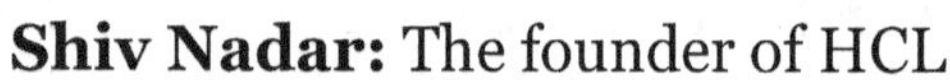 **Shiv Nadar:** The founder of HCL Technologies, a global IT services company, dropped out of college and started his career as a freelance computer programmer.

These are just a few examples of successful businessmen who did not have a college degree but were able to achieve great success through hard work, determination, and innovation.

Summary:

While having a formal education can be helpful, it is not a necessary requirement to succeed in business. Many successful business leaders and entrepreneurs did not have a college degree, and instead relied on their creativity, ingenuity, and hard work to achieve success. Some famous examples include Steve Jobs, Richard Branson, and Henry Ford. Ultimately, success in business depends on a variety of factors, including hard work, determination, and a willingness to take Risks.

Chapter-12

Self-Made Millionaires

Perhaps the most outwardly identifiable quality of self made millionaire people is action-orientation. They learn about a new method or technique and they tried it out immediately.

If they failed, if the new technique did not work, they tried it again and learned from it to become smarter and more competent. They would not loose. They took those practical proven methods, techniques, and strategies and apply them over and over - until they become one of the greatest sales professional of their generation.

Self-made millionaires are individuals who have accumulated a net worth of at least $1 million through their own efforts, rather than through inheritance or other forms of financial support. These individuals are often known for their entrepreneurial spirit, Risk-taking abilities, and strong work ethic. Many self-made millionaires come from humble backgrounds and have built their wealth through hard work, determination, and a willingness to take calculated Risks. Some common characteristics of self-made millionaires include a strong focus on goal-setting, a willingness to learn and adapt, and a disciplined approach to managing their finances.

In their book *The Millionaire Next Door*, Thomas Stanley and William Danco found that 79% of Self-Made Millionaire in America were entrepreneurs and sales people. It turned out that the most important skill for success is entrepreneurship and the ability to sell a product or service. Sales skills opened almost every door.

By the law of probability your ability to sell well moves you to the front of the line in terms of financial potential. The probability of your achieving financial independence, and even becoming a millionaire, is higher as a result of being better in sales than any other field. And there are no limits to what you can accomplish except the ones in your own mind.

Remember, no one is smarter than you and no one is better than you. Everyone starts at the bottom. Everybody who is doing well today was once doing feebly. And anything that anyone has learnt, you can learn as well. If someone is doing better than you, it is only because they have learned the key skills before you have. And the proof that you can learn those skills is that they have learned those skills, starting from nothing and knowing them in the first place.

Summary:

Self-made millionaires are individuals who have accumulated a net worth of at least $1 million through their own efforts, rather than through inheritance or other forms of financial support. They are known for their entrepreneurial spirit, Risk-taking abilities, and strong work ethic. These individuals often come from humble backgrounds and have built their wealth through hard work, determination, and a willingness to take calculated Risks. Characteristics of self-made millionaires include a strong focus on goal-setting, a willingness to learn and adapt, and a disciplined approach to managing their finances. Sales skills and entrepreneurship are identified as essential skills for success, and the ability to sell a product or service is emphasized as a key factor in achieving financial potential. The message is that everyone has the potential to become a successful self-made millionaire by adopting a positive mindset, learning key skills, and taking action.

Chapter-13

The law of 8

8 Undeniable Laws of High Performing Entrepreneurs

1. Your approach to work life balance makes a difference

Aditya Puri is a highly respected banker and former CEO of HDFC Bank, known for his disciplined work ethic and focus on customer service. His commitment to maintaining a healthy work-life balance is also noteworthy and serves as an inspiration to many.

According to his wife Anita Puri's recent interview on CNBC, Adiya Puri would always make time for his family and prioritize his personal life. He would come home for lunch at the same time every day at 1 pm, take a 10 minutes break to watch a Shammi Kapoor's movie to unwind from all the pressure in the bank, and then wrap up his office work before returning home in the evening sharp at 5:30 pm.

Ask him how he manages to leave office early every day and his reply is that people should just stop confusing working hard with working late. People stay back to please the bosses or, because they feel obliged to hang out with their colleagues. All this is a waste of time and an inefficient use of the organisation's resources, is Aditya's stock answer.

This kind of discipline and balance is essential for anyone seeking long-term success and happiness. By prioritizing his personal life and ensuring that he had time for family and leisure activities, Puri was able to maintain a sense of perspective and avoid burnout. Overall, Aditya Puri's approach to work-life balance is a great example of how successful professionals can achieve both their career goals and their personal aspirations.

Chaper-14

The law of 8

2. Taking care of your health

This law is followed by all these self-made millionaires.

Story of Rakesh Jhunjhunwala

It is difficult to find someone who does not know Rakesh Jhunjhunwala, an iconic figure and known as the Indian Warren Buffett. Starting with a meagre capital of Rs. 5000 borrowed from a friend, he built an empire worth Rs. 40,000 Crs. As most Indian investors, I was a hard-core follower and fan of Mr. Rakesh Jhunjhunwala when he died at the age of 62. During and after the budget session, I watched and heard him on CNBC. I was absolutely blown away by the investment advice he gave to the program viewers.

In one of the TV interviews, a beautiful anchor asked him, "What is his greatest regret in life?" How would he live his life if given the choice? "

Pat was the answer,

"As a result of my busy schedule and excitement to create further wealth, I completely neglected my health. I am willing to exchange my wealth for better health if it is feasible."

Rakesh Jhunjhunwala died at the young age of 62 and left behind a wealth of Rs. 40,000 Crs ($ 5000 Million).

The moral of the story is that health is the only thing that truly matters.

Mental, emotional, and physical health are your primary assets in life.

In order to make a sale, you need to demonstrate passion and vitality to your prospects when you are face-to-face.

When I was a child, my father would teach me the importance of taking care of one's health. One of his famous couplets read:

"Old age never goes away once it comes and

Youth never comes after lost."

It is imperative that you take care of your physical health. The more energy you have, the more quickly you will bounce back from rejections and failures. Your levels of self-confidence and self-esteem will be astronomical, and you will make a positive impact on everyone around you.

Preserve your health for your longer lasting jawani (youth).

The chances of your making a sale are ever so enhancing if you have bright and energetic in a sales conversation. The highest performance sales people are fastidious about their health and energy. They eat the right food, get lots of rest, and exercise rigorously

Many of the top paid CEOs across the world are Marathon runners e.g. The Chairman of the Board of Tata Sons, the holding company and promoter of more than 100 Tata operating companies with aggregate annual revenues of more than US $100 billion, Mr. Natarajan Chandrasekaran, he is a regular Marathon runner.

Why Taking Care of Your Body is Good for Health?

There are a number of reasons why taking care of your body is good for your health:

- **Health problems affect functioning**: Health problems, even minor ones, can interfere with or even overshadow other aspects of your life. Even relatively minor health issues such as aches, pains, lethargy, and indigestion take a toll on your happiness and stress levels.
- **Poor health habits can add stress to your life**: They also play a role in how well you are able to cope with stress. The stress that comes from poor health is significant.
- **Poor health interferes with daily living**: Health challenges also affect other areas of your life. Health problems can make daily tasks more challenging, create financial stress, and even jeopardize your ability to earn a living.
- **Stress can worsen health**: Stress itself can exacerbate health issues from the common cold to more serious conditions and diseases, so maintaining healthy habits can pay off in the long run.

It is important to remember that your prospect does not buy your product first. Instead, he always buys you. Ultimately, who doesn't prefer to work with someone who is a presentable personality and has a sharp mind?

Give it a try. There will be a noticeable difference right away.

Summary:

The law of 8 is followed by self-made millionaires and involves taking care of one's health, as exemplified by the story of Rakesh Jhunjhunwala. Jhunjhunwala, who built an empire worth Rs. 40,000 crores ($ 500 Million), expressed regret over neglecting his health and emphasized the importance of mental, emotional, and physical health as primary assets in life. Taking care of one's health can improve functioning, reduce stress, and prevent health problems that can interfere with daily living and earning a living. Additionally, maintaining healthy habits can pay off in the long run, as stress can worsen health issues. In sales, a presentable personality with a sharp mind is key, and taking care of one's health can enhance energy and vitality in sales conversations.

Chapter-15

The law of 8

3. Get lots of sleep

Most adults suffer from mild forms of sleep deprivations. They are not getting enough sleep each weeknight to perform at their best during the weekdays. Don't let this happen to you. Get to bed before 10 pm at least 5 nights per week and increase your sleep from 6 or 7 hours to 8 hours per night. You will feel amazed at the difference. Your physical and mental level of health will be of the highest order. Your personality will be more likeable.

Chapter-16

The law of 8

4. Be ambitious

Perhaps, the most important single quality that leads to high performance and sales success is ambition. To be ambitious, you must be hungry. You must have an intense, burning desire for sales success when the money that goes with it. You must get up each morning thinking, *I can hardly wait to get out there.*

Sales success comes from being eager to call on new prospects. When you see that by succeeding in sales you can achieve all your other goals, for yourself and your family, your level of ambition will increase to the point where you will become absolutely unstoppable. Ambition is a wonderful thing.

No Ambition, No Future.

On the other hand, there are people who are not particularly ambitious. Perhaps, selling insurance is not the right field for them. In many cases they have achieved a certain level, and they are complacent. They have adjusted their life styles to their current income and have no real desire to improve them in any way.

Even if you offer them prices and incentives, they are not motivated to work any harder than they already are. These people may be steady, average producers, but they have no real future in the world of competitive selling.

Summary:

The key to high performance and sales success is ambition. To be successful, you must have an intense, burning desire for sales success and be hungry for the money that comes with it. This eagerness leads to being eager to call on new prospects. Ambition is crucial to achieving all your other goals and becoming unstoppable. However, some people are not particularly ambitious and have no desire to improve their lifestyles or work harder, making them average producers with no real future in the competitive selling world.

Chapter-17

The law of 8

5. Sharpen your skills

Over the years, I have learnt that primary reason for failure in selling is that sales people simply do not know how to sell. They do not identify needs clearly. They do not present properly. They do not know answer objections intelligently. And they do not know how to follow up and close professionally.

As a result, they go from customer to customer but make few sales. All this can be overcome by improving your sales skills and increasing your level of determination.

I advise my students to do the followings:

a)   Subscribe and read Business Newspaper – like Economic Times, Wealth Magazine.
b)   Watch the interviews of the leading CEOs and Economist on various Business Channels like CNBC.
c)   Select your mentor with an utmost care and follow him to the hill.

"Often, I ask my students, "Who would you choose as a cricket coach for your child; a club level cricketer or an all-time great like Sunil Gavaskar?"

A Club Cricketer OR Sunil Gavaskar

The answer is obvious. Learn and follow the people who have actually achieved the great milestones in their lives.

Summary:

The fourth law for achieving sales success is to sharpen your skills. Many salespeople fail because they lack proper sales skills, such as identifying customer needs, presenting effectively, answering objections, and closing professionally. Improving these skills and increasing determination can overcome these shortcomings. To improve sales skills, it is advised to read business newspapers and magazines like Economic Times and Wealth Magazine, watch interviews of leading CEOs and economists on business channels like CNBC, and carefully select and follow mentors who have achieved great milestones in their lives.

Chapter-18

The law of 8

6. Be productive by spending more time on ...

Prospecting / Seeking Referrals

Make a decision today to work by Referrals only; ask each customers and non-customers / influencers who have a greater reputation in the society for the names of prospects you can talk to.

Resolve to sell by Referrals only

The highest paid sales people work on the basis of Referrals only. They make it a regular part of their sales work to ask for Referrals from anyone, everywhere they go. They have developed so many different contacts and sources of Referrals that they no longer have time to prospect for new business.

When you visit a referral from a happy customer, the sale is 90% made before you even open your mouth. This is the fastest and most predictable way for you to move into the top ranks of the highest income earners in your field. And the key ? **Just ask.**

Summary:

The above chapter discusses the importance of prospecting and seeking Referrals in sales. It suggests making a decision to work by Referrals only and asking each customer and non-customer/influencer for the names of prospects to talk to. The highest paid salespeople work on the basis of Referrals only, making it a regular part of their sales work to ask for Referrals from anyone and everywhere they go. When visiting a referral from a happy customer, the sale is already 90% made before even opening your mouth.

The key is simply to ask for Referrals.

Chapter-19

What is the best way to ask for Referrals?

Asking for Referrals can be a great way to grow your network, find new opportunities, or receive endorsements for your work. Here are some tips on how to ask for Referrals effectively:

Be specific: Clearly identify what you're looking for, whether it's a job opportunity, potential client, or an introduction to someone in your field. This makes it easier for the person you're asking to provide a relevant referral.

Choose the right person: Reach out to people who know you well, have had positive experiences working with you, and are well-connected in your industry. They'll be more likely to vouch for you and make meaningful connections.

Time it right: Ask for Referrals when your relationship with the person is strong and the timing is appropriate. Avoid asking during moments of high stress or when the person may be too busy to help.

Personalize your request: Tailor your request to the individual by mentioning shared experiences or specific reasons why you think they can help. This shows that you value their opinion and expertise.

Be polite and professional: Approach your request with a courteous and respectful tone. Make it clear that you understand they are doing you a favor and that you appreciate their time and effort.

Offer to reciprocate: If you can, offer to help the person in return by providing Referrals or support in their own endeavors. This shows that you're not just looking for a one-sided relationship.

Follow up: Once you've received a referral, follow up with a thank-you message to show your gratitude. Keep the person updated on the outcome of the referral, as they will likely be interested in your success.

Here's a sample template for asking for a referral:

Subject: Request for Referral – [Your Name]

Dear [Referrer's Name],

I hope you are doing well. I've recently been exploring new opportunities in [your field or industry], and I was hoping you might be able to help by providing a referral or introduction.

As we worked together on [specific project or experience], I believe you have a good understanding of my skills and expertise in [specific area]. I'm particularly interested in [specific type of opportunity or role] and thought you might know someone in your network who could benefit from my experience.

Of course, I'm more than happy to return the favour if there's anything I can do to help you in your own professional endeavours. If you have any questions or need more information, please don't hesitate to ask.

Thank you in advance for any assistance you can provide. I truly appreciate your support and the connections we've made.

Best regards,

[Your Name]

[Your Contact Information]

Summary:

The best way to ask for Referrals is to be specific, choose the right person, time it right, personalize your request, be polite and professional, offer to reciprocate, and follow up. When asking for a referral, it's important to clearly identify what you're looking for and tailor your request to the individual. You should approach your request with a courteous and respectful tone and offer to help the person in return. Finally, once you've received a referral, follow up with a thank-you message and keep the person updated on the outcome. A sample template for asking for a referral is provided.

Chapter-20

The law of 8

6. Be productive by spending more time on ……

a). Presentations

You must develop a unique style of presentation.

Present unique features of your plan and expand how do they differentiate from the plans of other sellers.

Present the price versus the value of your plan vis-a-vis your competitor's plan.

Be truthful. Never make a promise which you cannot fulfil. Remember, a successful sales person delivers what he promises.

Present joyfully and peacefully, knowing that the right thoughts and the right efforts will inevitably bring about right results.

A few tips to be an effective presenter are as under:

Be presentable: Your dress code, tidiness should be impeccable. Make a habit of wearing a Coat/ Blazer while on work.

Improve your personal traits and cultivate impeccable habits.

To be a successful sales person, dress appropriately and maintain a professional appearance.

Absolutely, maintaining a professional appearance and dressing appropriately is essential for a successful salesperson. Your appearance plays a significant role in creating a positive first impression, establishing credibility, and fostering trust with your prospects and clients. Here are some tips for ensuring a professional appearance as a salesperson:

Dress for your audience: Consider your industry, company culture, and the expectations of your clients when selecting your attire. In some industries, formal business attire may be expected, while in others, business casual may be more appropriate.

Clean and well-fitted clothes: Ensure that your clothes are clean, well-fitted, and in good condition. Ill-fitting, wrinkled, or damaged clothing can create a negative impression and detract from your professionalism.

Grooming: Maintain good personal hygiene and grooming habits. This includes regular showering, dental care, and grooming facial hair (if applicable). Keep your hair clean, neat, and styled in a professional manner.

Minimal accessories: Use accessories to enhance your professional appearance but avoid overdoing it.

Stick to simple, classic pieces that complement your outfit and avoid overly flashy or distracting items.

Appropriate footwear: Choose clean, well-maintained, and professional-looking shoes that match your attire. Ensure your shoes are comfortable, as you may need to stand or walk for extended periods during sales presentations or meetings.

Personal hygiene: Pay attention to personal hygiene, including using deodorant, maintaining fresh breath, and keeping nails clean and trimmed.

Subtle fragrances: If you choose to wear a fragrance, opt for a subtle scent that won't be overpowering or offensive to others.

Body language: Be mindful of your body language, including maintaining good posture, making eye contact, and offering a firm handshake. Your non-verbal cues can contribute to your overall professional appearance.

Adapt to the situation: Be prepared to adjust your appearance based on specific sales situations or client preferences. For example, if you are meeting with a more conservative client, you may need to dress more formally than usual.

By maintaining a professional appearance and dressing appropriately, you can create a positive impression, establish credibility, and foster trust with your clients, all of which are essential for a successful salesperson.

My father, who spent his entire career in the insurance industry, always advised me to eat what I liked and dress how other people like. It is imperative that you maintain a neat and tidy appearance at all times. Make sure you maintain a professional appearance. A blazer with or without a tie is a must. Maintain a clean and shiny pair of shoes. Your vehicle needs to be in pristine condition at all times. I promise that all of these things make a difference.

I want to share a real-life experience that happened to me when I presented a detailed Business Continuity Plan to an unknown HNI after a cold call. Over the course of three presentations, the HNI attentively listened to everything I said. At the end of the third meeting, I received a check for Rs. 38.00 lacs. I believed my presentation had been highly effective with him. However, when I asked him what he liked about my presentation, his response took me by surprise. He said, "Even though I didn't understand much of what you said, the way you spoke and your impeccable dress code instilled enough confidence in me to trust you." This incident highlights the power of appearance and presentation in making a strong impression on clients.

Your appearance and presentation make you so powerful as a result.

Smile and a firm handshake.

We are naturally drawn to people who smile and people may even assume you have more positive personality traits if you're smiling.

Research has shown that people who smile regularly appear more confident, are more likely to be promoted, and are more likely to be approached. Try putting on a smile at meetings and business appointments. You might find that people react to you differently.

When negotiating business agreements, a warm but strong handshake establishes trust and signals your willingness to negotiate. With a confirming handshake, you can make a good first impression at your business. You can acquire a client, by shaking hands strongly and confidently.

Summary:

The key to being productive in presentations as a salesperson is to develop a unique style and present the unique features of your plan, while being truthful and delivering what you promise. Dressing professionally and maintaining good personal hygiene is important, as it creates a positive first impression and establishes credibility and trust with clients. To maintain a professional appearance, consider the industry and client expectations, wear clean and well-fitted clothes, groom well, use minimal accessories, wear appropriate footwear, and pay attention to personal hygiene. A warm smile and firm handshake can also help establish trust and make a good first impression. A personal anecdote is shared to illustrate the impact of appearance and presentation on building confidence and trust with prospects.

Chapter-21

The law of 8

6. Be productive by spending more time on ......

b). Your introduction should consist of a 20-second benefit statement.

You should be brief, describing precisely what unique services you can provide your prospects in order to fulfill their unfulfilled secret desires (needs). Ideally, it should generate a lot of curiosity in your prospect, so he or she wants to meet you.

In the later part of this book, a Brief 20 second self introduction using Benefit Statements is provided.

Testimonials and their importance

Testimonials play a crucial role in building trust and credibility, both for individuals and businesses. They provide potential clients, customers, or employers with an unbiased evaluation of a product, service, or individual's skills and abilities. Testimonials can have a significant impact on decision-making processes and can sway opinions in favor of the person or organization being reviewed. Here are some reasons why testimonials are essential:

Social proof: Testimonials act as social proof, demonstrating that others have had positive experiences with a product, service, or individual. This validation can help establish credibility and trust, making potential clients or customers feel more confident in their decision to engage with the person or organization being reviewed.

Builds trust and credibility: Genuine, positive testimonials can help build trust and credibility by showcasing the real-world experiences of satisfied clients or customers. This can be especially important for new businesses or professionals looking to establish themselves in their respective industries.

Overcomes scepticism: Testimonials can help overcome scepticism by providing real-life examples of success and satisfaction. They can help alleviate concerns or doubts potential clients or customers might have before making a decision.

Highlights strengths and unique selling points: Testimonials can emphasize the strengths and unique selling points of a product, service, or individual, making it easier for potential clients or customers to understand what sets them apart from their competitors.

Enhances online presence: Positive testimonials on websites, social media platforms, or review sites can improve a company's or individual's online reputation, making them more appealing to potential clients, customers

How to collect Testimonials?

Collecting testimonials can be a valuable way to showcase your work and build credibility. Here are some strategies for gathering testimonials from your clients, customers, or partners:

Ask for feedback: After completing a project or delivering a service, reach out to your clients or customers and ask for feedback. Request that they share their experiences, focusing on the positive aspects of your work. Be polite and let them know how much you appreciate their feedback.

Use surveys or questionnaires: Create a short survey or questionnaire to gather feedback from your clients or customers. This can be a convenient way for them to provide testimonials, as they can fill out the form at their leisure. Be sure to include open-ended questions that encourage detailed responses.

Leverage social media: Monitor your social media profiles for positive comments, reviews, or mentions. When you find one, ask the person if you can use their comment as a testimonial on your website or marketing materials. Alternatively, you can create posts asking your followers to share their experiences with your product or service.

Request video or audio testimonials: Some people may prefer to provide testimonials in video or audio format. These can be more engaging and persuasive than written testimonials, as they convey emotions and authenticity more effectively. Ask your clients or customers if they'd be willing to record a short video or audio clip sharing their experience.

Gather testimonials at events: If you host workshops, seminars, or other events, set up a testimonial booth where attendees can share their experiences on camera or in writing. This can be an excellent opportunity to collect testimonials in person and in a more casual setting.

Make it easy.

Summary:

To be productive, spend time on crafting a 20-second benefit statement for your introduction that highlights your unique services and generates curiosity in your prospect. Testimonials are essential for building trust and credibility, and they provide social proof and overcome skepticism. Testimonials can be collected by asking for feedback, using surveys, leveraging social media, requesting video or audio testimonials, or gathering testimonials at events. Making it easy for clients to provide testimonials is key to successfully collecting them.

Chapter-22

The law of 8

6. Be productive by spending more time on ......

Closing Sales

You should know how to answer objections and close the sale. In big ticket sales where the premium value is very high prospects prefer to take some time to consult with the in-house or other experts. They like to do their entire homework by consulting with their existing insurance sellers and the similar plans offered by the other insurance companies.

During this waiting period often the insurance seller gets a bit nervous and jittery. He thinks that he has meticulously followed the entire process of sales, the presentation gone very well and at the end of presentation he could feel the positive vibe coming around. He believes that the sale is almost done and that he would receive a call from the prospect anytime soon. However the reality is different. For days together he does not receive any communication from the prospect and this makes him more unrestful as he has no clue as to how he should proceed which can help closing the sale without sounding salesy or pushy.

Friends, this is a very common phenomena and I am sure the readers must have passed through the similar phase sometime or the other.

Value Letters:

One of the most effective ways to keep in touch with your prospect and creating an impression that you are a unique seller commanding deeper knowledge and experience is to write powerful value letters from time to time which can help him to separate you from the crowd.

Double your productivity, double your income

Your ability to manage your time can be a critical factor in your success as a sales professional. The quality of your time management often determines the quality of your life.

Remember, salespeople only get paid for results. The only food you can eat is what you kill, as they say in hunting.

Since you only get paid for results, don't do anything that does not pay.

No matter how many things you do in a week or a month, there are only 3 activities that pay you your desired income. These 3 activities account for more than 90% of your income. The secret to sales success, or success in any field, is this;

Do more and more of fewer things, but more important things and get better and better at each of them.

In selling, no matter what the product the only 3 activities that will pay your desired income are

Prospecting,

Presenting, and

Closing

Only when you are engaged in these core activities are you actually working. A sales person remains unemployed until he gets face-to-face with someone who can and will buy within a reasonable period of time. Only then the work day begin.

One of the simplest ways for you to double your income is to double the amount of time you spend prospecting, presenting and closing.

Summary:

To close a sale, it is important to know how to answer objections and address the concerns of potential customers. In big-ticket sales, customers often take time to consult with in-house or other experts before making a decision. During this waiting period, it can be challenging for salespeople to stay motivated and not come across as pushy or salesy.

One effective way to stay in touch with prospects and demonstrate expertise is through value letters. These letters can help set you apart from the competition and keep you top of mind with potential customers.

Time management is also critical for success in sales. Salespeople only get paid for results, so it's important to focus on the three core activities that generate income: prospecting, presenting, and closing. Doubling the amount of time spent on these activities can significantly increase income. The key is to do more of fewer, more important things and continuously improve in each area.

Chapter-23

The law of 8

7. Be a good human being

What is the true definition of success?

Win their Trust and Likeability

The true definition of success is not just about achieving financial prosperity, but also about being a good human being.

Remember, winning over the Trust and Likeability is the corner stone of selling Big insurance policies to HNIs. Based on my years of experience I observed that the prospects seldom understand the entire content of your presentation. Instead they look at your body language and the confidence that you display during the course of discussion and make a judgement.
It is said that a prospect first buy a seller and then his plan.

The only way you can achieve the above state of your body and mind is by being a good human being who believes in utmost honesty and putting the interests of the buyer before his personal priority.

All those selling tricks and smartness of selling a comb to a bald person simply do not work for long. It is said that you can fool somebody for once but you can't fool everybody forever.

A highly successful insurance agent keeps customer's interests in forefront, never over promises and believes in delivering in time what has been promised.

This is indeed the foundation of creating a successful empire. I would, therefore, strongly advice all those new generation young advisors to strictly follow this path. They may initially find it difficult to follow what has been advised but believe me there is no other way out. Just continue to do it persistently keeping utmost faith in oneself and God.

Summary:

The true definition of success encompasses not only financial prosperity but also being a good human being. Winning the trust and likeability of clients is crucial when selling large insurance policies to HNIs. Prospects often focus on body language and confidence during presentations rather than the content itself.

Achieving this state of mind and body requires honesty and prioritizing the interests of the buyer above personal gains. Traditional selling tricks and deception don't yield long-term results.

A successful insurance agent prioritizes customers' interests, avoids overpromising, and delivers on commitments promptly. This approach forms the foundation of a thriving business.

Young advisors should adhere to these principles, even if it's challenging at first. Persistence, faith in oneself, and belief in a higher power will ultimately lead to success.

Chapter-24

The law of 8

8. Success is a function of your ability to manage your time

Your ability to manage your time can be a critical factor in your success as a sales professional. The quality of your time management often determines the quality of your life.

Success is indeed influenced by one's ability to manage time effectively. Time management is a crucial skill that can impact various aspects of life, including professional achievements, personal growth, and overall well-being. Here are some reasons why time management is essential for success:

Prioritization: Effective time management involves prioritizing tasks based on their importance and deadlines. This helps ensure that essential tasks are completed on time, contributing to overall productivity and goal achievement.

Efficiency: Time management skills enable individuals to work more efficiently, maximizing their output within the limited time available. This can lead to increased productivity and the ability to accomplish more in a shorter period.

Goal setting: Setting ambitious goals and creating plans to achieve them is a key aspect of time management. By breaking down larger objectives into smaller, manageable tasks, individuals can make steady progress toward their goals.

Stress reduction: Poor time management can lead to increased stress levels due to missed deadlines and an overwhelming workload. By managing time effectively, individuals can reduce stress and maintain a healthier work-life balance.

Work-life balance: Effective time management allows individuals to allocate time for both professional and personal activities, contributing to a balanced and fulfilling life. This balance can promote overall well-being and long-term success.

Focus and concentration: Time management techniques, such as blocking out distractions and setting aside designated periods for specific tasks, can improve focus and concentration. This increased focus can lead to higher-quality work and greater overall productivity.

Adaptability: Strong time management skills enable individuals to adapt to changing circumstances and prioritize tasks accordingly. This adaptability can help maintain productivity and progress toward goals, even when faced with unexpected challenges or setbacks.

In nutshell, success is significantly influenced by one's ability to manage time effectively. By prioritizing tasks, setting goals, maintaining focus, and striking a balance between professional and personal life, individuals can enhance their productivity and increase their chances of achieving their desired outcomes.

Summary:

Effective time management is crucial for success in various aspects of life, including professional achievements, personal growth, and overall well-being. Prioritizing tasks, working efficiently, setting realistic goals, reducing stress, maintaining a work-life balance, improving focus and concentration, and being adaptable are some of the key benefits of time management. By managing time effectively, individuals can enhance their productivity and increase their chances of achieving their desired outcomes.

Chapter-25

Set high goals

"The greater danger for most of us isn't that our aim is too high and miss it, but that it is too low and we reach it."

- **Michaelangelo**

Michelangelo di Lodovico Buonarroti Simoni, known as Michelangelo, was an Italian sculptor, painter, architect, and poet of the High Renaissance. Born in the Republic of Florence, his work was inspired by models from classical antiquity and had a lasting influence on Western art.

Life Insurance

Despite the fact, there are 24 life insurance cos. are in existence the insurance penetration is abysmally low. Insurance penetration in India experienced an increase in momentum in recent years moving to 4.2% in 2021 from 3.76% of GDP in FY20.

There is potential for selling big ticket insurance to high net worth individuals. Wealthy HNIs, who have accumulated wealth in recent years, are struggling with a sense of insecurity.

How can you set timid goals in an industry with a low penetration rate and an economy that will grow exponentially in the coming decades?

As I can clearly see, the growth prospects are enormous.

Low goals are self-destructive.

It is for this reason that most insurance agents fail.

Summary:

The quote by Michaelangelo reminds us of the importance of setting high goals and reaching for them. In the life insurance industry, despite the presence of 24 companies, insurance penetration in India is still low. However, there is a huge potential for selling big ticket insurance to high net worth individuals who are looking to protect their wealth. In this industry with significant growth prospects, setting low goals is self-destructive and a common reason why many insurance agents fail. It is important to set high goals and work towards achieving them.

Chapter-26

A set of sure-fire questions that will open the doors to HNIs

Insurance products aren't easy to sell to someone who is already wealthy. You can't sell them by telling him how much money they could make by buying an insurance product.

You have to sell them beyond the concept of making money.

Fear Analysis:

To become Rich, you must solve the unsolved problems of Rich men.

You need to get into their inner circle, understand their unresolved concerns, and offer them solutions that are unique.

Remember that the only reason HNIs are going to buy insurance from you is that they believe their problems are getting solved and that doing so will benefit them more than not doing so.

Selling insurance is essentially a Risk Management process. Identify Critical Risks that HNI faces in the current era and offer unique solutions which are difficult to ignore/deny.

Introduce yourself as Risk Manager in lieu of Insurance Seller/ Advisor.

A set of sure-fire questions that will open the doors to HNIs.

1. Have you hedged your Personal Guarantees?

2. Have you created a firewall to protect the Enterprise value of your Business?

3. Do you have a comprehensive Financial Business Continuity Plan?

Need Analysis:

Since the time immemorial the life insurance is sold with the help of need analysis of a human being. As far as HNIs are concerned, this is a redundant concept since they do not have any traditional needs. In that case how do you sell life insurance to them. Let me explain to you further.

Bread, Clothes, and a Roof over your head are the basic elements of need. In addition, you can include Children's Education, Marriage, Retirement, and Annuities.

However, when we are trying to analyze the need of HNIs who have amassed tons of wealth during their lifetime the above-made definition of need is out of place. In any case, they have made adequate provisions with sufficient reserves that will cover such needs in case of an eventuality.

It is then necessary to determine whether they have any other kind of need. Yes, they do have needs in the form of aspirations and mitigations of their personal pain points.

I will explain it to you in more detail.

In simple terms, human beings have two basic aspirations in their lives:

1. Creating a large amount of wealth.
2. To protect the wealth they have earned.

To the extent that these needs are not met, they are called aspirational needs. The pain points they experience are called personal pain points.

You can be a big success in selling life insurance by providing solutions to HNIs' unfulfilled aspirations and pain points.

Summary:

The chapter discusses the challenges of selling insurance products to high-net-worth individuals (HNIs) and suggests a set of questions to open doors to such individuals. The chapter emphasizes the need to understand the HNIs' unresolved concerns and offer them unique solutions. It suggests positioning oneself as a Risk Manager rather than an insurance advisor and identifies risk management as the essence of selling insurance. The chapter explains that traditional needs analysis may not work for HNIs who have already made adequate provisions to cover their traditional needs. Instead, it is essential to determine their aspirational needs and personal pain points and provide solutions accordingly. The chapter concludes that successful insurance sales to HNIs require selling large insurance policies and addressing their unfulfilled aspirations and personal pain points.

Chapter-27

You need to identify your customers

Who could be my Client? Define them.

If you can't define them you can't find them. Be very specific as to who are your customers.

Make sure you get clients you want to work with

Working with a client you don't like is one of the worst things about being an insurance agent...

Most of us have experienced nightmare clients at some point in our lives.

One of the main reasons why you get these nightmare clients is that you're stuck selling in a highly competitive niche.

These kinds of clients only look for the cheapest deal with rebates and will shop around until they get it.

But it doesn't have to be this way...

Most agents tend to take on any client they can because they believe they are the only ones available...

If this describes you...

Unfortunately, you don't have a system to target only high-quality leads who would be perfect clients for you.

As opposed to a **sniper approach**, you're taking a **shotgun approach** and taking anything and everything instead of carefully selecting your targets.

The good news is that you don't need to do this anymore...

That's why we teach you the concept of **"6 Filters"** to select the quality of clients that you should have.

It is these types of clients that you actually want to work with.

6 Filters that describes the quality of customers you need to have:

1. Proprietary / Partnership /Pvt. / Public Ltd. Companies / High Earning Individuals
2. Preferably Well – Qualified 1st Generation Entrepreneur
3. Profit Making Organization
4. Willingness to Take Risks
5. Having Secured Liabilities / Personal Guarantees
6. Age- Around- 45 with reasonably good health.

I would love to work with the people like these-

Zerodha founder Directors set for Rs. 100 Cr ($13.33 million) Annual Salary.

There was a news item in all business magazines that caught the attention of many. Zerodha is an Indian brokerage company founded by three young promoters in Bengaluru. They have become India's number one brokerage company in just 10-12 years.

The three young founders/directors each raised their salaries to Rs 100 Cr ($13.33 million) per year.

It's just another news story for many. I see this as a wonderful opportunity to sell insurance exceeding Rs. 100 Cr ($13.33 million) each.

Be a part of the ecosystem of high net worth individuals. Gain their trust and likeability. I promise, as they become richer, so will you.

Summary:

The chapter emphasizes the importance of identifying and targeting specific customers to achieve success in the insurance industry. It advises insurance agents to define their ideal customers and focus on targeting high-quality leads rather than taking on any client they can get. The chapter provides "6 Filters" to select the quality of clients that agents should work with, such as preferring well-qualified 1st generation entrepreneurs, profit-making organizations, and individuals with a willingness to take risks. It also suggests targeting high net worth individuals, citing the example of the three young founders/directors of

Zerodha who each raised their salaries to Rs 100 Cr ($13.33 million) per year as an opportunity to sell insurance policies exceeding that amount. The chapter emphasizes the importance of gaining the trust and likeability of high net worth individuals to achieve success in the insurance industry.

Chapter-28

Effectively prospecting for big insurance policies among HNIs

Prospecting high net worth individuals (HNIs) for selling big insurance requires a targeted and sophisticated approach. Here are some of the best ways to prospect HNIs:

Build a strong network: Networking is key to accessing HNIs. Attend events, conferences, and seminars where HNIs are likely to be present. Join clubs, associations, and groups that cater to affluent individuals to expand your connections.

Develop strategic partnerships: Collaborate with professionals who cater to HNIs, such as wealth managers, financial planners, private bankers, real estate agents, and attorneys. These partnerships can provide valuable referrals and introductions to HNIs.

Utilize social media platforms: Leverage social media platforms like LinkedIn, Facebook, and Twitter to connect with and engage HNIs. Share valuable content, offer insights, and showcase your expertise in insurance solutions for affluent individuals.

Content marketing: Establish yourself as a thought leader in the insurance industry by creating informative and engaging content, such as blog posts, whitepapers, podcasts, or webinars. Target topics that are relevant to HNIs, such as wealth preservation, estate planning, and risk management.

Provide exceptional service to existing clients: Satisfied clients can be your best advocates. Offer outstanding service to your current clients, and encourage them to refer you to their high net worth friends, family, and colleagues.

Offer exclusive events and seminars: Organize events, workshops, or seminars tailored to HNIs to educate them about the benefits of big insurance and how it can protect their wealth. These events can also serve as networking opportunities, helping you build relationships with potential clients.

Target niche markets: Identify and target niche markets within the HNI segment, such as entrepreneurs, professionals, athletes, or celebrities. Specializing in a specific niche can help you differentiate yourself from competitors and demonstrate your expertise.

Leverage public records and databases: Use public records, databases, and online tools to identify and research potential HNI prospects. Look for information on real estate holdings, business ownership, and philanthropic activities to gain insights into their financial profile and interests.

Personal branding: Develop a strong personal brand that reflects your expertise, credibility, and commitment to serving HNIs. This can help you build trust and rapport with potential clients.

Follow up and nurture leads: Regularly follow up with your prospects and nurture relationships over time. Provide valuable information, insights, and updates to stay top of mind and demonstrate your commitment to helping them protect their wealth.

Remember, prospecting HNIs for big insurance requires patience, persistence, and a long-term approach. Focus on building relationships and demonstrating your expertise to earn their trust and ultimately win their business.

Summary:

Prospecting high net worth individuals (HNIs) for selling big insurance requires a targeted approach that includes building a strong network, developing strategic partnerships, utilizing social media, creating engaging content, providing exceptional service, organizing exclusive events, targeting niche markets, leveraging public records, developing a personal brand, and nurturing leads. Patience, persistence, and focusing on building relationships and showcasing expertise are key to earning HNIs' trust and winning their business.

Chapter-29

Change your business model – Don't put all your eggs in 1 basket – Expand your Products Offer

It is your Dharma (duty) to offer your clients the best need-based product available anywhere in the universe.

It will be fallacy not to offer the better product to your prospect offered by any other institution just because you are not connected with that institution.

Offer All Financial Products. Ensure that your hard-earned HNI prospects are not knocking on your competitor's doors to obtain products you don't offer.

Enlarge the size of your organization. Enter into a joint venture with the people who are expert in different domains. Ensure that your revenue continue to flow from different products. You always have a greater degree of success when you have enough products in your basket supported by the expert advice.

I have personally witnessed many examples of successful insurance agents cross-selling all other financial products. Multiplying your income this way is the easiest and most effective method.

Your order of priority in terms of offering products to them should be as under:

1. Health Insurance

- Andrew J. Scott

According to Andrew J. Scott, a Professor of Economics at the London Business School, children born today could potentially live up to 100 years. In 2023, the current life expectancy for India is 70.42 years, which has been steadily increasing over the years. By 2050, the average life expectancy in India is projected to surpass 80 years, with the country's population reaching 1.7 billion and the majority of people falling within the working age group of 15 to 64 years.

India's increasing life expectancy can be attributed to advancements in medical care, improved diets, and healthier lifestyles. In 1950, India's life expectancy was only 35.21 years, but it is expected to reach 81.96 years by 2100.

These developments have important implications for both individuals and financial advisors:

As people live longer, they may need to consider postponing their retirement or ensuring that they have a suitable source of passive income during their retirement years. This could involve saving more, investing wisely, or planning for alternative income streams.

Health insurance becomes even more crucial for every Indian, given the ever-rising medical expenses. Living without health insurance could be financially devastating, especially as healthcare costs continue to increase.

Financial advisors and professionals selling financial products should prioritize offering health insurance and retirement planning products to their clients. These products are essential to address the evolving needs of individuals as they live longer, healthier lives.

By focusing on these key financial planning areas, individuals can better prepare for a longer life expectancy and ensure their financial stability in their later years.

Why Health Insurance? – Huge Under Penetration/ Increase in awareness / Corona Factor

Though there has been a rise in demand for health insurance products, India continues to have the highest levels of under-penetration in the world, with only 0.16% of the total population insured for health, as per IRDA. Little wonder then that 70% of healthcare expenses are met from one's pocket.

The health insurance is a first product you should discuss with your client and ensure that he/she has made adequate provision of a sufficiently large amt. of health insurance with unique features and least no. of exclusions.

The minimum ticket size of the health insurance offered by you should be Rs. 50.00 Lacs and above when you are selling insurance to HNIs.

You can create huge value for your clients by judiciously combining the Deductible amount and Super Top Up plan as shown in the following table.

e.g. for a person aged 35 covering 4 family members

Plan	S. A.	Deductible	Premium + GST
Basic	Rs. 5.00 Lacs	Nil	Rs. 20055
Super Top Up	Rs. 50.00 Lacs	Rs. 3.00 Lacs	Rs. 18950

Top-up plans: High protection, low cost

HEALTH PLAN	COVER SIZE (₹)	ANNUAL PREMIUM (₹)
Base plan	5 lakh	8,102
Super top-up plan	25 lakh with 5 lakh deductible	1,646
Base + Super top-up plans	5 lakh + 25 lakh	9,748
Higher base plan	25 lakh*	14,626

For 35-year-old male in Delhi, without discounts. | * Option for ₹30 lakh not available.
Source: Niva Bupa Health Insurance.

You are helping your prospect to increase his protection cover for the least amount of premium by adding this value addition.

In addition to gaining their trust and likeability, such value additions open the doors to HNIs.

Selling Health Insurance creates a win-win situation and, therefore, it must be on your selling bucket list.

2. Protection Insurance

Why is it necessary to take Protection Insurance? Be it personal or Business Insurance

Insurance serves as a form of risk management. Its purpose is to provide financial protection and peace of mind in the event of unfortunate incidents, unexpected events, accidents, or disasters that could cause significant financial strain or loss. Here's why it's important for both individuals and businesses:

Personal Insurance:

Life Insurance: Provides financial support to your dependents if you die prematurely.

Health Insurance: Protects you from the high costs of healthcare. Hospital stays, medications, and treatments can be expensive and insurance can mitigate these costs.

Auto Insurance: If you own a car, insurance will cover the costs associated with car accidents, including repairs, and in some cases, medical expenses.

Homeowners/Renters Insurance: Protects your home and belongings from disasters like fires, theft, and natural disasters. It also provides liability coverage if someone is injured on your property.

Disability Insurance: Offers income protection if you become unable to work due to injury or illness.

Business Insurance:

It provides an adequate cover to hedge

i). Institutional Secured Liabilites / Personal Guarantees given by the Directors.

ii). Enterprise Value of the Business.

iii). Business Continuity Plan.

Directors and Officers Liability Insurance: Directors and Officers (D&O) Liability insurance is a coverage designed to protect directors and officers of a company or other types of organizations from personal liability in the event they are sued for alleged wrongful acts in managing the company. These acts may include fraud, misuse of funds, misrepresentation of assets, breach of fidiciary duty, and others. D&O insurance covers defense costs and financial losses but typically does not cover fines, penalties, or legal fees resulting from criminal proceedings.

General Liability Insurance: Protects your business from financial loss resulting from claims of injury or damages occurred on your business property.

Property Insurance: Covers your business property and assets (like equipment, inventory, etc.) in the event of a loss due to fire, theft, or other disasters.

Workers Compensation Insurance: Covers medical treatment, disability, and death benefits in the event an employee is injured or dies as a result of their work.

Business Interruption Insurance: If your business operations are interrupted due to a covered loss, this insurance helps cover your lost income to keep your business viable.

Remember, insurance doesn't prevent bad things from happening, but it can make recovery from those situations much more manageable by mitigating the financial risk. The exact insurance you need can vary depending on your specific circumstances, such as your location, type of business, personal health, and so on.

3. Retirement Planning

Why is it necessary to have retirement planning at an early age?

Retirement planning is a key aspect of long-term financial planning and stability. Here are several reasons why it is crucial to start retirement planning at an early age:

Compound Interest: The earlier you start saving, the more time your money has to grow. Compound interest allows your savings to increase exponentially over time, so starting early can lead to significantly larger retirement savings.

Higher Risk Tolerance: When you start investing early, you generally have a higher risk tolerance because you have more time to recover from any potential losses. This allows you to invest in higher-risk (and often, higher-return) investment vehicles that can significantly grow your retirement fund.

Financial Security: By starting early, you can ensure you have enough money to maintain your desired lifestyle during retirement. Many people underestimate the amount they will need, so starting early helps ensure you have sufficient funds.

Increased Life Expectancy: As healthcare improves, people are living longer, meaning retirement funds need to last longer. By starting to save early, you can accumulate more to support these additional years.

Uncertain Social Security: The future of social security benefits can be uncertain, and relying solely on these for your retirement can be risky. Having personal retirement savings can provide additional security.

Higher Cost of Living: Inflation causes the cost of living to rise over time. By starting your retirement planning early, you can better prepare for these increased costs in the future.

Financial Independence: Retiring early or achieving financial independence is more attainable if you start saving at an early age.

Less Financial Burden: Starting early means you can contribute smaller amounts regularly over a longer time span instead of larger amounts later on, which could potentially burden your finances.

Healthcare Costs: Healthcare can be expensive during retirement, and having a robust retirement fund can help ensure you can afford any necessary treatments or care.

Remember, retirement planning is not just about saving money, but also about understanding how to invest and increase your wealth over time. It often involves strategic planning with respect to investment, tax planning, and understanding your retirement goals and desires.

4. Accidental Insurance

What is accidental benefit?

Definition: Accidental death benefit and dismemberment is **an additional benefit paid to the policyholder in the event of his death due to an accident**. Dismemberment benefit is paid if the insured dies or loses his limbs or sight in the accident.

Do we need personal accident insurance?

**Yes, a Personal Accident cover is mandatory
for all two-wheelers**. The same can be bought
along with your two-wheeler insurance policy.

Look at the entire gamut of benefits available under a
typical accidental insurance

   i) Partial and total Disability Benefits;
  ii) Accidental Hospitalization;
 iii) Air Ambulance Cover
 iv) Children Educational Benefit
  v) Coma due to Accidental Bodily Injury
 vi) Fracture Care
vii) Hospital Cash Benefit
viii) Loss of Income due to disability from accident.
 ix) Loan Protection Cover
  x) Road Ambulance Cover
 xi) Travel Expenses Benefits

**All you need to pay is Rs. 2,600 pm for
Accidental Insurance of Rs. 2.00 Cr along with
the following benefits :**

1.   A huge partial and total disability benefits (Rs.
2.40 Cr)

2.   Accidental Hospitalization Expenses (Rs. 5.00
Lacs)

3.   Coma due to Accidental Bodily injury (Rs. 10.00
Lacs)

4.   Fracture care (Rs. 1.00 Lacs)

To my mind this insurance is a must for every person
and in case you are not offering you are doing a great
dis-service to your prospect. My advice is don't look at

your personal earnings and think only from the view point of your prospect's interest.

5. Micro Insurance

These low-value products, which no one sells, will set you apart from the crowd and serve as an entry point to building relationships with HNIs. This method has worked for me and I have achieved incredible results.

How many of you are aware of the micro-insurance available in the market?

Here are some examples of extremely low-cost and high-value products:

1. Student's Safety Insurance
2. Dog Insurance - Kennel Club
3. Extended Warranty Insurance
4. Kidnap and Ransom Insurance
5. Art Insurance
6. Pedal cycle Insurance
7. Cyber Security Insurance
8. Mobile Insurance
9. Cab Ride Insurance
10. Group Medical Insurance Plan
11. Group Term Plan
12. Bharat Laghu Udhyam Plan

Mobile Insurance:

• More than 7.5 Lacs mobile phones are sold every single day.

• More than 60% of them are Smart phones.

- Only fraction of them are being insured.

- Smart phone may cost Rs. 10,000 to Rs. 1.00 Lac and above.

It covers damages, technical malfunctioning, pick up and drop facilities.

Cyber Security Insurance:

Phishing is the most prevalent cyber scam. This is increasing at the rate of more than 500%. It covers the individual and organization both.

Scope of Coverage

- Hacking your Bank A/C.
- Personal Letters.
- Impersonation.
- Legal Cost.

Cab Ride Insurance:

- Very low premium insurance.

- Covers baggage loss.

- Home burglary.

- Missing your flight.

You can open the doors of HNIs with these great products and gain the trust and likeability of your customers.

Here's a real-life story about how one of my students won the trust and likability of an unknown HNI, which eventually led to a big insurance sale.

Mrs. Zora's cherished dog, Ratan, played a pivotal role in helping Deepak achieve MDRT status with a single policy. Are you curious to learn how?

Here's the story:

Deepak Chaudhary, a 35-year-old life insurance sales advisor, had eight years of experience under his belt. Despite working hard and receiving guidance from various trainers, MDRT qualification eluded him. Driven by his ambition to succeed in life insurance sales, Deepak continually sought to improve his skills.

After attending a Masterclass of mine titled "Sell 22 Policies to HNIs and Secure Your Financial Future," Deepak was inspired to join my comprehensive training sessions. Owing to his keen learning ability, he quickly grasped how to secure appointments with unknown HNIs and design irresistible offers for them, excelling in the use of micro insurance.

During the training, we taught Deepak to build a network of influencers connected to HNIs. He delivered an impressive presentation on Risk Management to this group, introducing himself as a

Risk Manager. His presentation won their confidence, and they provided valuable references. Leveraging a 20-second benefit statement, Deepak easily scheduled appointments with these HNIs.

One of the references was Sohrabjee, a wealthy Parsi real estate businessman. He lived with his wife Zora, daughter Rubi, and their beloved Pomeranian, Ratan, who was adored by the entire family. Deepak diligently researched the family, learning about their hobbies and gathering information about Ratan.

In the first meeting, Deepak initiated a conversation by asking general questions about Sohrabjee's life, business, fears, aspirations, and plans for risk mitigation. He promised to develop a tailored Business Plan to help Sohrabjee create and protect his wealth and requested a follow-up appointment.

As the meeting concluded, Deepak observed Ratan approaching Mrs. Zora with enthusiasm. Recognizing the family's affection for their pet, Deepak inquired about Ratan and shared pictures of his own dog, creating a friendly atmosphere.

In the subsequent meeting, Deepak presented Sohrabjee with a detailed business plan encompassing risk management solutions and investment options. The plan stood out due to the personalized touch of including Ratan, such as suggesting a life insurance policy for Sohrabjee with a rider covering Ratan's medical expenses in emergencies.

Sohrabjee was impressed by Deepak's personalized approach and purchased the proposed policy, which not only helped Deepak achieve MDRT status but also led to referrals from Sohrabjee's HNI circle.

In essence, Deepak's success highlights the importance of personalizing services and building emotional connections with clients in the life insurance industry. It's about understanding their needs and providing customized solutions that help them reach their objectives.

<u>**Innovative Message to act as a Lead Magnet**</u>

Sub: You are about to discover secrets of 12 low priced Protection Gears that 99% people are not aware of. Yes. This will add Huge Value to your Life and Business.

Dear,

Sorry to abruptly land in your inbox.

I just wanted to inform you that sometime in the rush of business life we fail to appreciate the values and the utmost needs of some protective gears around us.

These are –

1. Student's Safety Insurance
2. Dog Insurance - Kennel Club
3. Extended Warranty Insurance
4. Kidnap and Ransom Insurance
5. Art Insurance
6. Pedal cycle Insurance
7. Cyber Security Insurance
8. Mobile Insurance
9. Cab Ride Insurance
10. Group Medical Insurance Plan
11. Group Term Plan
12. Bharat Laghu Udhyam Plan

These absolutely Unique / Low Priced Protection Gears have potentials to add immense values in your Personal and Business lives.

We are champions in assessing the needs and the amount of protection that you and your organization may need.

Sounds Interesting?

Call us / Reply Back NOW…

Summary:

The author suggests changing the business model by expanding the products offered and not relying on just one type of product. The author suggests offering all financial products and partnering with experts in different domains to ensure a revenue flow from different products. The author recommends offering health insurance, protection and retirement planning as the first products to discuss with clients due to the high under-penetration in India. The author also suggests offering accidental insurance and micro-insurance, which includes low-value products that are not typically sold but can set agents apart from the crowd and serve as an entry point to building relationships with high net worth individuals. The author provides a real-life example of an agent using micro-insurance to win the trust and likeability of an unknown high net worth individual, which led to a big insurance sale. The author suggests using personalized attention and building emotional connections with clients to make a difference in the insurance industry. The author concludes with an innovative message to act as a lead magnet for prospective clients.

Chapter-30

Set your priorities Right

Remember, your loyalty towards your hard earned customers should be 100% and nothing less than that. Their interest should be your prime objective and certainly more than your earnings in short term gains. Sell the products which are best to fulfil their needs in a best possible manner.

There is no harm in offering the products of other insurance companies if you think they are superior in terms of fulfilling your prospects needs and aspirations.

This will certainly build up their Trust and Likeability and will clearly work as a road-map for unprecedented success in future.

This mantra will surely give you magical results!!!

Create Value – Think of giving before you demand in order to create value

Remember, HNIs will only buy from you when they

a)   Know you.
b)   Like you
AND
c)   Trust you.

Do not forget as an advisor our currency is Trust. Never Manipulate. Only influence.

Instead of asking for business, identify their pain points and offer solutions.

One would wonder what could be the fear/pain points of such highly affluent people surrounded by all affluence and amenities.

Since time immemorial, every human being has strived to become richer quickly and to maintain / save and protect their wealth as they accumulate it. It is a constant fear of losing everything they have earned during their lifetime that keeps them awake at night.

The only way one can make HNI to do what you want them to do is by giving them what they want.

What do they want?

Deep – Rooted secret desires

Following are the needs/ deep-rooted secret desires of HNIs: -

A. Wealth Creation
B. Wealth Protection- Mitigating Critical Risks.

This in turn would mean providing need based solutions to the following:

1. Adequate Financial Protection that can mitigate their Personal /Business Risks.

2. Asset Allocation from the viewpoint of Wealth Management.

3. Review and reshuffle the investments to optimize Returns.

4. An assurance that their Assets are performing well and giving Returns higher than Inflation Rates.

My personal experience has shown that the following are the major fears/pain points of such affluent people:

a). Hedging the Personal Liabilities and Guarantees offered to Financial Institution.
b). Covering a Succession Risk and Protecting the Enterprise Value of the Business.
c). A comprehensive Financial Business Continuity Plan which can fulfil their aspirations even in their absence.

Providing solutions to mitigate their fear/pain points will certainly add a great deal of value to their lives.

You will be welcomed with both hands open. There will be no problem getting an appointment with them.

This is something I have personally experienced.

Each time I present my concept; my prospects appreciate it and often offer to hire me as a consultant.

Think about how this could happen in an era when insurance agents offer huge rebates.

Our job is to educate/help them to achieve their goals by designing customized financial plans for them.

Rebrand yourself as

 "Risk Managers"

Instead of Insurance Advisors.

"You can have everything in life you want if you just help other people get what they want.'

-       **Zig Ziglar**

Summary:

The key to success in selling insurance to HNIs is to prioritize their needs and interests above your own short-term gains. Offer a range of financial products, and focus on creating value for your clients by identifying and solving their pain points. HNIs' deep-rooted secret desires include wealth creation and wealth protection, which can be achieved through adequate financial protection, asset allocation, investment review, and financial business continuity planning. As a "Risk Manager," rather than just an insurance advisor, you can build trust and likeability with your clients and gain their loyalty by providing customized solutions to their financial needs.

Chapter-31

Skip the "icebreaker" step with prospects

One of the hardest parts of working with new prospects is getting them past the "icebreaker" phase.

They have no idea who you are...

They have no idea what you can do for them...

They're likely already on the defensive because of all the other scammy agents that give our industry a bad name.

And despite all this we need to get them to trust us so we can help them with their insurance needs.

So what can we do about it?

It's actually very simple.
Use the followings as a part of your tool kit while you are facing your prospect for the first time.

1.   **Your 20 Sec Benefit Statement**

Value Proposition
(Introduction)

Hello, my name is ...

As a dedicated group of Corporate Risk Managers, our mission is to assist individuals in optimizing and safeguarding their wealth by minimizing associated risks.

Our approach?

We meticulously identify the critical risks within your business, quantify their potential impact, and develop a tailored Financial Business Continuity Plan to mitigate these threats. This empowers you to enjoy a life with significantly reduced risk.

Please take a moment to explore our organization's details further.

==> http://randhirbhallaandassociates.com

The three phrases in this statement possess a captivating effect:

Risk Manager

Wealth Creator

Wealth Preservation Advocate

Why do I consider these phrases magical?

From personal experience, I've noticed that incorporating these three terms in my introductory statements has piqued the interest of 7 out of 10 new prospects. They are eager to learn more about what I've briefly mentioned.

Moreover, these prospects have been willing to schedule appointments with me.

Showcase my Books, Videos, Profile, and Testimonials

During my initial presentations, I present my books available on Amazon, YouTube videos, and a comprehensive profile along with testimonials. This solidifies my credibility in the minds of new prospects, making them more receptive to my message.

Incorporate these ice-breaking strategies when engaging with new prospects regularly.

I can assure you that this approach will set you apart from the typical insurance seller. By establishing trust even before their first appointment, you'll create a unique and positive experience for your prospects.

Summary:

Overcoming the "Icebreaker" Hurdle with Prospects

One of the most challenging aspects of working with new prospects is moving past the "icebreaker" phase, when they have no idea who you are or what you can offer. They may already be on the defensive due to other unscrupulous agents in the industry. Despite this, we need to build trust to help them with their insurance needs.

The solution is simple: use the following tools when meeting prospects for the first time:

Your 20-Second Benefit Statement

Introduce yourself with a value proposition that highlights your role as a Risk Manager, Wealth Creator, and Wealth Preservation Advocate. This captivating approach has been proven to generate interest and appointments from 7 out of 10 new prospects.

Showcase Your Books, Videos, Profile, and Testimonials

During initial presentations, display your books, videos, profile, and testimonials to establish credibility. Regularly incorporating these ice-breaking strategies will set you apart from typical insurance sellers and create a unique, positive experience for your prospects by building trust before their first appointment.

In summary, overcome the icebreaker hurdle by presenting a strong value proposition and showcasing your credibility, which will ultimately lead to increased interest and trust from prospects.

Chapter-32

You cannot believe in God until you believe in yourself

"You cannot believe in God until you believe in yourself."

-Swami Vivekananda

To end this book, I would like to use a quote from Swami Vivekanand, one of the greatest spiritual leaders India has ever produced.

It is undeniably necessary to believe in oneself and in the almighty God in order to achieve great success.

Furthermore, the quote by Swami Vivekananda emphasizes the importance of self-belief in one's spiritual journey. It suggests that having faith in oneself is a prerequisite to having faith in a higher power. Let's explore this concept further.

Self-awareness: Believing in yourself requires self-awareness, which means understanding your strengths, weaknesses, and motivations. When you know yourself well, you can better comprehend your place in the world and your relationship with a higher power.

Inner strength: Believing in yourself fosters inner strength, resilience, and self-confidence. When you trust your abilities and judgments, you can face challenges with courage and conviction. This inner strength enables you to maintain faith in God during difficult times, as you understand that you possess the ability to overcome obstacles.

Spiritual growth: As you believe in yourself and cultivate self-confidence, you begin to recognize your true potential and purpose in life. This realization encourages spiritual growth and a deeper understanding of your connection with God.

Empowerment: Believing in yourself empowers you to take control of your life and make choices that align with your values and beliefs. When you trust your instincts and follow your own path, you can achieve a more authentic and fulfilling spiritual journey, strengthening your faith in God.

Personal responsibility: When you believe in yourself, you accept personal responsibility for your actions and their consequences. This sense of accountability is crucial for spiritual growth, as it enables you to learn from your mistakes and make amends, fostering a deeper connection with God.

Humility: Believing in yourself doesn't mean being arrogant or self-centered. Instead, it involves recognizing your own worth while remaining humble and open to learning from others. This humility allows you to appreciate the vastness of God's wisdom and the limits of human understanding.

In conclusion, Swami Vivekananda's quote highlights the significance of self-belief in developing a strong spiritual foundation. By believing in yourself, you can cultivate self-awareness, inner strength, spiritual growth, empowerment, personal responsibility, and humility. These qualities ultimately enhance your faith in God and help you to lead a more meaningful and purposeful life.

Chapter-33

Recap

How to make a million dollars in the insurance business

My confession before I conclude this book is that making a million dollars in the insurance business requires a lot of hard work, dedication, and persistence. Here are some strategies that may help:

Specialize in a niche market: Find a specialized market within the insurance industry that you can excel in, such as healthcare or cyber liability insurance. By focusing on a specific field such as HNIs, you can become an expert in that field and attract clients who value your knowledge.

Build a strong network: Networking is essential in the insurance business. Build strong relationships with clients, industry professionals, and referral sources. Attend industry events, join relevant associations, and use social media to connect with potential clients and industry influencers.

Offer superior customer service: Focus on providing exceptional customer service to your clients. By delivering a high level of service, you can build trust, loyalty, and Referrals from satisfied clients.

Leverage technology: Use technology to streamline your operations, improve your customer service, and reduce your costs. Invest in customer relationship management software, automation tools, and other technologies that can help you work more efficiently and effectively.

Continuously educate yourself: Keep up with the latest trends, regulations, and developments in the insurance industry. Continuously educate yourself by attending seminars, training programs, and other educational events to stay ahead of the competition.

Set ambitious goals: Set ambitious goals for yourself and your business. Create a detailed plan with specific targets and milestones that you want to achieve, and work diligently towards those goals every day.

Remember that making a million dollars in the insurance business takes time, effort, and a lot of hard work. But by following these strategies, you can increase your chances of success and achieve your financial goals.

Prepare to elevate your skills and reach new heights with our comprehensive program

Our Ultimate Sales Skills (USS) Training Programs

In this book, you've merely glimpsed a single droplet, but there is an entire ocean waiting for you to explore. Immerse yourself in our Ultimate Sales Skills (USS) Training Programs to dive deeper into this world.

What can you expect to gain from this program?

Our program primarily emphasizes innovation, aiming to inspire the transformations you desire. We'll equip you with exclusive tools and techniques taught at the world's leading business schools.

Drawing from my extensive 45-year corporate journey, I will share invaluable knowledge and insights to help you grow.

Prepare to elevate your skills and reach new heights with our comprehensive program.